The Life, Times & Music® Series

JAZZ DUETS

The Life, Times & Music® Series

ANDREW G. HAGER

FRIEDMAN/FAIRFAX

PUBLISHERS

A FRIEDMAN/FAIRFAX BOOK

ISBN 1-56799-359-1

Editor: Tony Burgess
Art Director: Jeff Batzli
Designer: Stephanie Bart-Horvath
Photography Editor: Kathryn Culley
Production Manager: Jeanne E. Hutter

Grateful acknowledgment is given to authors, publishers, and photographers for permission to reprint material. Every effort has been made to determine copyright owners of photographs and illustrations. In the case of any omissions, the publishers will be pleased to make suitable acknowledgments in future editions.

Color separations by HK Scanner Arts Int'l Ltd.
Printed in Hong Kong and bound in China by Midas Printing Limited

For bulk purchases and special sales, please contact:
Friedman/Fairfax Publishers
Attention: Sales Department
15 West 26th Street
New York, NY 10010
212 685-6610 FAX 212 685-1307

Visit the Friedman/Fairfax Website: http://www.webcom.com/friedman/

CONTENTS

INTRODUCTION

The great duets of jazz reflect in words and music how drastically the United States has changed over the last one hundred years. As the voices of black and white men and women rose together across the airwaves, sharing a new American musical language called jazz, the myth of inherent human inequality began to be put to the test. For the first time in history, it became apparent that people of all colors and of both sexes could not only survive, but also thrive together.

At first an instrumentalist's form, jazz used improvisation to express the idea that musicians could offer new and ever-changing melodic structures within the confines of the age-old song forms. Jazz entertained audiences, but more importantly, it relayed the

Louis Armstrong and Velma Middleton hamming it up. The pair performed together for ten years.

crucial musical message that each member of a community has the right and the responsibility to express himself or herself with clarity and purpose.

Although vocalists were virtually excluded from early jazz, they eventually played a large role in the popularity of the music. By gaining the attention of music lovers who were more accustomed to lyric storytelling, vocal jazz helped expose an ever-widening audience to instrumental improvisation.

Few of the partners who recorded duets together had more than a brief professional relationship, having been brought together by their labels or by producers of movie musicals. The handful of singers who did have ongoing working relation-

ships have, for the most part, passed on, leaving the details of their relationships to the imaginations of adoring fans.

To understand how the vocal duet became part of the music, it is important to understand how jazz evolved from a variety of popular musical idioms: the blues, gospel, European song form, and the Broadway musical. Once singers became stars in their own right, they introduced the duet into the jazz repertoire. Though very few of the participants in recorded duets knew each other personally, the singers' true characters often evoked the com-plexities of fragile human relationships.

Thanks to the advent of record-ing, radio, and mass distribution, the impact of jazz has not been lim-ited to the boundaries of North America. Respected and revered for its musical and sociological achieve-ments, jazz is now practiced in nearly every country around the world.

As singer Jimmy Rushing once put it, in the thirties and forties nearly every male singer was either "a high Bing or a low Bing." Everyone took a distant second (or third or fourth) to Crosby during his reign.

THE EVOLUTION OF THE SINGER

B efore offering their gifts to jazz, American vocalists practiced several different music traditions. Blues singers, minstrels, and Broadway performers had the most notable impact on the evolution of the jazz singer.

The Blues

Rooted in the African-American slave culture of the southern United States, the blues can best be described as the secular kin to black gospel music. Based on the "flatting" of the fifth tone of the eight-note scale, the blues has played a key role in nearly every form of American popular music in the twentieth century.

Since most of African-American history and culture was not recorded during the two hundred and fifty years of slavery, it is nearly impossible to attach specific names and stories to the true roots of American blues. The story as it can be documented begins with the end of slavery in the 1860s, when many in the first generation of freedmen earned meager livings as minstrels in vaudeville and in medicine shows.

Charley Patton, who originally worked at the Will Dockery Plantation, was one of a handful of musicians credited with popularizing the Delta blues.

A large percentage of the early professional blues and minstrel entertainers who first came to national attention were from the Mississippi Delta region. The Will Dockery Plantation, located outside of Cleveland, Mississippi, was home to some of the most famous early practitioners of the blues.

Charley Patton (1887–1934), whose recordings on Paramount made him one of the first nationally recognized blues singers, lived and worked for some time on the Dockery farm, along with other notable performers, such as Willie Brown (1900–1952), Howlin' Wolf (1910–1976), and Roebuck "Pops" Staples (b. 1915).

Mamie Smith (1883–1946) is credited with the first blues hit, "Crazy Blues," recorded and released by OK/Phonola in 1920. Other female blues stars who emerged during the 1920s included vaudeville performers Gertrude "Ma" Rainey (1886–1939) and Ida Cox (1898–1967).

Thanks to the blues, theater and music professionals shared a common musical language from 1920 on, a language that included both lyrical narrative and innovative instrumentation, setting the stage for the birth of the jazz vocalist.

African-American Theater

African-American minstrel and medicine show performers—as well as the white performers who mimicked them—played a large role in the evolution of vocal jazz. Many of the singers who participated in early African-American musical theater were able to parlay their successes into healthy recording careers, permanently linking the history of popular song form, its singers, and instrumental jazz.

According to the Census Bureau, by 1890 there were 1,490 black actors touring with minstrel companies across the United States. Bessie Smith (1898–1937), W. C. Handy (1873–1958), and Bert Williams (1877–1922) were just a few of the black entertainers who honed their skills on the minstrel and vaudeville circuits. Although the road for black performers was rough, their mounting success with white audiences made their presence on Broadway inevitable.

Even though white Americans had an interest in black entertainment, as evidenced by the "blacking up" of white performers, during the teens only one show written and performed by African-Americans, *All Coons Look Alike To Me,* by Ernest Hogan, was produced in New York (off-Broadway). It was not until Noble Sissle (1889–1975) and Eubie Blake's (1883–1983) *Shuffle Along* achieved its astounding

540-performance run in 1921 that musicals written and performed by blacks gained broad recognition. The show's instantaneous and overwhelming success spawned more than just the hit song "I'm Just Wild About Harry"; it dispelled once and for all the misperception that white audiences wouldn't go to see entertainment written and performed by blacks. *Shuffle Along* spawned a decade of successful African-American musicals, created the first black stars, and, as Langston Hughes pointed out, ignited the Harlem Renaissance. (Hughes also claimed that he decided to attend Columbia University so that he'd be able to see Sissle and Blake's show).

The first black stars created by the shows that followed in the footsteps of *Shuffle Along* were predominantly blues performers. Ethel Waters (1896–1977) appeared in two

The Empress of the Blues, Bessie Smith, died from survivable injuries sustained in a car accident after the Mississippi hospital she was rushed to refused to admit her because she was black.

The first generation of internationally recognized African-American stars, including Paul Robeson, Josephine Baker, Florence Mills, and Adelaide Hall, came from the ranks of black dancers, singers, and actors who contributed to the success of *Shuffle Along*.

very successful shows, *Oh Joy* and *Cabin in the Sky*; Edith Wilson (1896–1981) and Florence Mills gained fame in *Plantation Revue*; Eva Taylor (1895–1977) had a hit with *Bottomland*; and the great Alberta Hunter (1895–1984) scored with the musical *Change Your Luck*. Although the syncopated music they were performing on America's stages and radios was closer to ragtime than jazz, the uniquely American sound of these black performers had been finally and wholly embraced by the white, entertainment-hungry public.

Noble Sissle and Eubie Blake, creators of the groundbreaking show *Shuffle Along*.

THE BIRTH OF JAZZ

Within a relatively short period of time, two similar schools of black music, ragtime and dixieland, laid the groundwork for new musical experimentation. Coming from different parts of the country and developing from different musical backgrounds, the practitioners of these two styles took advantage of many of the rhythms and improvisations of African music and the music of the southern plantations in developing a musical style that was uniquely American. As these seminal musicians continued to break new musical ground, a new, highly improvisational, free-wheeling form of music developed, which became known as jazz.

Ragtime

Ragtime music was born in saloons and bordellos, and it was a big part of what made the Gay Nineties sound so gay. In its classic form, it is instrumental piano music characterized by highly intricate syncopated melodies set against a straight march-type, or *oompah*, bass line. It usually consists of three or four distinct sections, or themes, each a self-contained entity made up of sixteen measures. After breaking onto the scene in the 1890s, piano ragtime was adapted into ragtime songs, music for small combos and brass bands, ragtime waltzes, and novelty rags. At the heart of all these variations

One the most crucial elements in the rise of jazz was the stride piano school, a combination of European and African techniques with which James P. Johnson is partially credited.

is the ever-present syncopation that gave ragtime, or "ragged time," its name.

The ragtime craze hit full stride during the first fifteen years of the twentieth century, becoming—along with its Tin Pan Alley variants, vocal and novelty ragtime—the most popular form of music in the world.

While literally hundreds of itinerant musicians—led by the great Scott Joplin (1868–1917)—are responsible for the phenomenon of ragtime music, the transition from ragtime into jazz is primarily credited to three specific composers, each of whom, in his own way, took ragtime beyond its established borders, introducing stylistic variations that would eventually come to be associated with jazz. The most notorious of these leaders was pianist, pool hustler, and sometime pimp Jelly Roll Morton (1890–1941), who maintained all his life that he had been the true "inventor" of jazz. W.C. Handy (1873–1958) was another, and though he himself never claimed to be the inventor of jazz, his admirers made the claim for him, dubbing him the "Father of Jazz." James P. Johnson (1894–1955), the third of these influential innovators, is less often recognized for his contribution, but his unique "stride" style of piano playing did much to set the stage for the complex bass lines characteristic of later jazz music.

When his song "The Entertainer" was used as the theme song to the movie *The Sting,* Scott Joplin, the most well-remembered composer of ragtime tunes, enjoyed a huge resurgence of popularity fifty-six years after his death.

Jelly Roll Morton (1890–1941)

Born Ferdinand Joseph LaMenthe, Jelly Roll Morton was the Creole son of one of the wealthiest businessmen in New Orleans. Eventually, however, he adopted his stepfather's surname of Morton. Being part of the upper-class Creole culture (a blend of French, African-American, and Native American blood), Jelly's early musical training was primarily classical European. He studied the violin, guitar, trombone, and, beginning at the age of eleven, the piano. All of these lessons were taught to him in his first language, French.

At the age of fourteen and after his mother's death, Jelly began playing piano in various seedy establishments in Storyville, the New Orleans Tenderloin district. His godmother never approved of music as a profession, let alone her godchild's fraternization with "hoodlums." Sometime between 1905 and 1907, Jelly's godmother kicked him out of the house, and he began traveling from state to state as an itinerant piano player and pool hustler. During the teens, Jelly worked in New York, Louisiana, Texas, and Chicago, and on the West Coast, but it wasn't until 1923 that Morton began his recording career with the all-white New Orleans Rhythm Kings in what may have been the country's first interracial recording session. While these Rhythm Kings recordings were not commercially successful, Jelly did record nineteen seminal piano solos in Richmond, Indiana, for the Gennett label around the same time. Between 1926 and

1930, Morton recorded nearly ninety sides with his studio group, called Jelly Roll Morton and His Red Hot Peppers.

Morton's personal style (flashy clothes and a diamond-inlayed tooth) and musical dexterity provided a provocative balance between art and entertainment, making him

A gregarious character and brilliant musician, Jelly Roll Morton has served as perfect fodder for plays, movies, and dozens of books.

one of the most popular entertainers of the 1920s. As the decade ended, however, the audience that had made him the king of ragtime and early jazz moved on to newer, more dance-oriented jazz, leaving Jelly Roll penniless and nearly forgotten.

Out of Morton's fifty-one years on this earth, only about three were spent in the limelight. His final two decades were spent in failed lawsuits and attempts at a comeback. Until the day he died, Jelly Roll Morton told anyone who'd listen that he alone had invented jazz.

W.C. Handy (1873–1958)

W.C. Handy was one of the first musicians to meld elements of blues song form with ragtime instrumentation. By doing so, Handy carved out one of the first clear paths to vocal jazz.

After attending Kentucky Music College, Handy began his professional music career in 1896 as bandmaster of a touring group called the Mahara Minstrels. His first hit song, "Memphis Blues" (originally entitled "Mr Crump" for the political campaign of E. H. "Boss" Crump), brought Handy to national attention in 1912. Handy recorded his most famous song, "St. Louis Blues," in 1914. This early blues classic was re-recorded by Louis Armstrong several times throughout Satchmo's long career. During the 1920s, Handy gave up life on the road and settled in New York City, where he worked as a music publisher. By 1940 he had lost his sight, but he continued to work at his Broadway office until his death in 1958.

James P. Johnson (1894-1955)

Stride, a style of piano playing based on complex rhythmic bass patterns played with the left hand, played an important role in the development of ragtime and jazz. The humble and nearly forgotten father of the Harlem, or East Coast, stride piano school was James P. Johnson. Like Morton, Johnson was a student of both European and African-American musical forms. His compositions featured a combination of gospel, southern blues, shouts and stomps, and European classical music styles, and provided a cornerstone for the growing American sound. His most famous hit, "Charleston," was one of the most popular songs of the Roaring Twenties. Johnson also wrote several symphonies, concertos, and tone poems, as well as an opera and the musical *Runnin' Wild,* a sequel to *Shuffle Along.*

Little is known about the personal life of the soft-spoken Johnson. The date of his birth is still disputed—James himself believed he was born on February 1, 1894, while his brother, years after Johnson's death, said he was "sure" James was born in either 1891 or 1892. From the 1940s on, he composed only sporadically, and made few recordings. A series of strokes ultimately left him paralyzed and bedridden until his death in November 1955, at his home in Jamaica, Queens, New York.

If not for the talent and tutelage of King Oliver, Louis "Satchmo" Armstrong would not have become one of the world's brightest entertainers.

Dixieland

Dixieland is a style of brass-oriented early jazz developed largely in New Orleans. "Dixie" was a nickname for New Orleans coined from a locally issued pre-1860 ten-dollar bill that had the French word "dix" (meaning "ten") on it. The early practitioners of the New Orleans sound had a profound influence on the development of American popular music, and their work in both nightclubs and vaudeville theaters inextricably links them to the rise of vocal jazz.

The first nationally recognized figure of the dixieland scene, Joseph "King" Oliver (1885–1938), was born on a plantation near Abend, Louisiana. He moved to New Orleans as a child to work as a "yard boy." While in New Orleans, Oliver studied both the trombone and the cornet. In 1907 he joined the Melrose Brass Band, and in 1912 he began to work with the Olympia Band. By 1915 Oliver's talent and hard work had earned him the position of bandleader.

Like many blacks of the early twenties, Oliver made his way to Chicago, where he found his greatest following as the bandleader of The Creole Jazz Band, which included Louis Armstrong (1900–1971), Armstrong's future wife Lil Hardin (1898–1971), and the famous clarinetist Jimmie Noone (1895–1944). He and the band made their first series of recordings in 1923. These seminal recordings were the first ever by an African-American jazz group, and provided some of the best examples of the New Orleans style of jazz.

In the early 1930s, severe dental problems forced "King" Oliver to stop playing the cornet. After a few recordings where he served solely as bandleader, Oliver retired to Savannah, Georgia.

His influence on the preceding and most well-known generation of dixieland players is undeniable. Of his protégés, the most popular was Louis Armstrong, who as a teenager had followed "King" Oliver from gig to gig. In Armstrong's autobiography, *Satchmo*, Louis makes no bones about his musical and personal debt to Oliver, stating that "King" was his first and only musical mentor.

Over the course of his career, Armstrong worked with dozens of female vocalists. Velma Middleton (1917–1961), for one, had the good fortune to be hired by Armstrong in 1942 to perform on tour and record with his band. From their collaboration came several popular recordings, the most successful of which was a duet called "All That Meat and No Potatoes," a comical number that highlighted the pair's stagey, vaudeville-style relationship.

After years of success as the front man for his own groups and as a member of other musicians' orchestras, Louis Armstrong put together the All-Stars, a group of musicians he toured with for more than ten years. Velma Middleton was Armstrong's singing sidekick for most of those years.

THE BIG BANDS

Ivie Anderson toured and recorded exclusively with Duke Ellington from 1931 to 1942. Her first hit with Duke, "It Don't Mean a Thing (If It Ain't Got That Swing)," recorded nearly two years prior to the swing craze, heralded the coming of this new style.

The golden era of the jazz vocalist came with the rise of the big band. Over nearly three decades, these orchestras went through a variety of changes, all of which had an impact on the evolving role of singers.

As jazz became more popular, and therefore capable of sustaining financially a greater number of players, bands became increasingly large. During the early thirties many of these bands began calling themselves "orchestras," which allied them closely with European music traditions. Aside from the name change, the music itself made more use of European musical theory, relying on intricate arrangements and orchestrations. The change gave an increasing number of musicians an opportunity to explore musical improvisation while remaining within the stricter European context.

African-American composers and arrangers continued to broaden the boundaries of American music during this time by studying and incorporating musical elements of European composers such as Debussy. By doing so, Duke Ellington (1899–1974), Johnny Mercer (1909–1976), and, later, Charles Mingus (1922–1979) created new, groundbreaking, and extremely melodic sounds for the big bands.

Until the invention and mass production of the microphone, singers were unable to hold their own as soloists among the inherently loud brass instruments. Yet, as early as 1918 vocalist-instrumentalists made their appearance as part of the brass, reed, and rhythm sections of the band, hired to handle the vocal refrains between instrumental solos. Joseph C. Smith's orchestra was one of the first big bands to include a vocal refrain in a jazz recording when the bandleader hired the trio of Harry McDonough, Charles Hart, and Lewis James to sing the refrain of Smith's popular composition "Mary."

After the invention of the microphone, singers were finally able to be heard while singing at a more subtle volume, and began their invaluable contribution to the development of jazz. One of the most popular of the early jazz singers was Cliff Edwards (1895–1972), who began his career in the teens working as an accompanist for silent movie houses. Edwards, also known as "Ukelele Ike," created a body of unusual vocal sound effects, which he termed "eefin'." These effects are the earliest recorded examples of scat

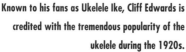

Known to his fans as Ukelele Ike, Cliff Edwards is credited with the tremendous popularity of the ukelele during the 1920s.

singing. The introduction of the microphone allowed him to make even greater vocal leaps and craft more unusual tones without having to strain his voice. His first recording, James P. Johnson's "Old Fashioned Love," showed off his vocal dexterity thanks to an opening "trumpet" solo. Edwards's vocal imitation of the horn was understandably mistaken by many people for the real thing. Although Edwards's contribution to early jazz is virtually forgotten, his later work in film, especially as Jimminy Cricket

Bing Crosby (1904–1977) and The Andrews Sisters

From the 1920s until his death in 1977, Harry Lillis "Bing" Crosby's ease with the microphone and conversation-volume singing voice made him the most copied singer of his day. Singers of the dance band era were, as singing legend Jimmy Rushing (1902–1972) once stated, either "a high Bing or a low Bing."

So too the work and overwhelming popularity of The Andrews Sisters—Laverne (1915–1967), Maxene (b.1918), and Patti (b.1920)—led to a string of female vocal groups trying to cash in on their singular craze. Bing and the sisters worked together throughout their careers to bring America hit after hit.

Their collaboration began with a rendition of "Don't Fence Me In," recorded in 1944 for the movie *Hollywood Canteen*. For the next twenty years, The Andrews Sisters sang back-up and shared lead vocals on dozens of tunes for Crosby's financially suc-

cessful albums, including "Pistol Packin' Mama," "Is You Is Or Is You Ain't My Baby," and "Ac Cent Tchu Ate The Positive." Although less memorable, other songs like "The Three Caballeros," "Along the Navajo Trail," "Jingle Bells," and "Sparrow In the Treetop" also graced the charts.

The Andrews Sisters began their career in the early thirties as a vaudeville team, and soon began working regularly with the Larry Rich Band. After moving to New York City for an extended booking at the Hotel Edison, the trio signed with Decca Records. Nearly overnight the sisters had their first smash hit with "Bie Mir Bist Du Schön," a Yiddish song from 1933 that they performed with a new set of Americanized lyrics by Sammy Cahn (1913–1993).

From then on the hits kept coming. "Hold Tight, Hold Tight" and "Roll Out the Barrel," to name just two, made the Andrews family indespensable in the entertainment industry. In

With the help of the Andrews Sisters, Bing Crosby met with some of his greatest musical successes, the most memorable of which is "Ac Cent Tchu Ate The Positive."

Harry Lillis "Bing" Crosby (middle) began his professional singing career as a member of the Rhythm Boys, a trio which also included Harry Barris (left) and Al Rinker—the brother of singer Mildred Bailey (pictured on the following page).

1940 the trio went to Hollywood and appeared in their first movie, *Arabian Nights,* with the Ritz Brothers. Soon thereafter they were put together with Crosby. The sisters also backed a number of other big name music makers, including Guy Lombardo (1902–1977), Ernest Tubb (1914–1984), Burl Ives (1909–1995), and Carmen Miranda (1909–1955).

Crosby's dream wasn't always a life in music. In fact, it wasn't until he began studying law at Gonzaga College in Spokane, Washington, that he started entertaining the idea. While in school he met Al Rinker, his future trio partner in the Rhythm Boys, and formed a group for which he played the drums and sang. The duo began working on the western vaudeville circuit in 1927, and soon made their way to Los Angeles. It was in the City of Angels that Harry Barris joined the Rhythm

Boys, and together the trio landed a gig with the famous Paul Whiteman Orchestra. From the fame he gained with the Whiteman orchestra as a member of the Rhythm Boys, Bing Crosby struck out upon a solo career as both an actor and singer. Like The Andrews Sisters, Bing collaborated with numerous other singers both on film and in the recording studio. One of the most popular of his duets, "An Apple For the Teacher," came from film work with the leader of the Boswell Sisters singing trio, New Orleans native Connee (1907–1976).

Both The Andrews Sisters and Bing Crosby are best known as popular music entertainers, although their early careers included substantial jazz recordings with legends like Bix Beiderbecke (1903–1931), Frankie Trumbauer (1901–1956), the Dorsey Brothers, and Duke Ellington.

Despite the childlike sincerity of her singing voice, Mildred Bailey gained a reputation as a consummate professional, respected and at times feared. Although she was one of the most popular singers of the day, Bailey died penniless at the age of forty-four.

singing "If You Wish Upon a Star," brought him to national attention and, in turn, nurtured the continuing relationship between the musical and jazz.

Again in the 1920s, trumpeter, singer, and bandleader Louis Armstrong made his mark on music, this time by nearly single-handedly legitimizing the pop-jazz singing school. Armstrong's 1926 hit "Heebie Jeebies" was so popular that, within a few months after its release, bandleader Paul Whiteman introduced a vocal trio to his staff of musicians. The group, known as the Rhythm Boys, was made up of singers Al Rinker, Harry Barris, and Harry Lillis "Bing" Crosby.

Before the rise of Bing Crosby as a solo artist, the most influential and notoriously unmusical talent manager-producer of early jazz, Jack Kapp, took a chance and placed singer Mildred Bailey (1907–1951) (the sister of Rhythm Boy Al Rinker) in front of the Casa Loma Orchestra. The four popular songs she and the orchestra performed consisted of fully sung verses bridged by eight-bar instrumental solos. Kapp had long held the belief that if female singers were able to become stars in their own right, the value of the band as a whole would naturally multiply. Proof of Kapp's hypothesis soon followed when Bailey had her first hit, "Rockin' Chair," which she recorded under the auspices of the Paul Whiteman Orchestra. Bailey's first successful solo effort marked the begining of America's twenty-year love affair with both the male and female jazz singer.

Shantootsies of the Thirties

As the female club singer, or *chanteuse* as she is called in French, developed into a star, her presence in the national media began to have an overwhelming impact on the perception of women in society. The image of the female jazz singer, dressed to the nines and emanating a taboo sexual energy, was a far cry from the woman's typical role in society as wife and mother.

Lee Wiley (1915–1975)

Unlike Mildred Bailey or the Boswells, Lee Wiley's greatest contribution to female vocal music was her heart-wrenching honesty—a quality that left the listener suspecting that she had led a very hard life. Her penchant for the hard truth, couched in seduction, made her quite successful; it also made her one of the earliest examples of the torch-song singer. Her work moved from pop-oriented songs to jazz-orchestrated show tunes. In doing so, Lee Wiley's music explicitly evoked the historic link between female jazz singing and its roots in musical theater. Wiley also helped invent the idea of the jazz "standard" with her Liberty recordings of the hits of Cole Porter, George Gershwin, and Rodgers and Hart.

During her long and prolific career, Lee Wiley performed with such jazz greats as Bud Freeman, Max Kaminsky, Fats Waller, Bobby Hackett, and Eddie Condon.

The Boswell Sisters

The music of the Boswells—Martha (1908–1958), Vet (1909–1988), and Connee (1907–1976)—was a product of their hometown of New Orleans and their upbringing in a musical family. Their mother, father, aunt, and uncle (the two women were sisters and the men brothers) sang in a quartet, which the Boswell children began to emulate from an early age. The sisters learned to play a number of instruments, including the cello, saxophone, violin, banjo, and piano.

Having lost three other siblings to illness and war, the Boswell family became inseparable. The harmonies that the original Boswell band and then the Boswell sisters moved toward were indicative of their devotion to one another. It is important to note that in the history of trio and quartet singing only two groups besides the Boswells were able to achieve the technical synchronicity worthy of consideration as vital to the evolution of jazz. Of the two other important groups, it is no surprise that the Mills Brothers were also family. The only other major trio, Lambert, Hendricks and Ross, didn't come along for another nineteen years.

The Boswell Sisters—Connee, Martha, and Vet—are best remembered for their tight harmonies and clever arrangements, both of which are evident in their hit song "Shout, Sister, Shout."

Crooners of the Thirties

The term "crooner," from the German word *kronen*, literally means to mourn or groan. Originally used as a derogatory description of the pre-microphone breed of American male singers, the term "crooner," like the word "jazz" (which originally described the music in brothels), survived its original negative connotation and eventually came to stand positively for the unique vocal work of twentieth-century popular American male singers.

The first American singer to be dubbed a crooner was pop idol Rudy Vallee (1901–1986), who came to national attention on the *Heigh-Ho Club Radio Hour* in 1927. As bandleader, saxophonist, and singer for a gang of Yale alumni called the Connecticut Yankees, Vallee gained popularity with "Vagabond Lover," a song that he cowrote and performed for the movie of the same name. From that point onward, Vallee himself was known as the "Vagabond Lover."

With the assistance of a band he put together as a student at Yale, Rudy Vallee became the first American singer to be dubbed a crooner.

The most popular singer of 1931, Russ Columbo was known for both his voice and his "Valentino" good looks.

Though Vallee was preceded by the likes of Cliff Edwards (1895–1972), the Vagabond Lover's success over-shadowed the popular-ity of his predecessors and ushered in the era of singers as stars. Although Vallee acknowledged his luck with the ladies, his success had more to do with phonetics than with his persona. By making use of a megaphone Vallee became, in his own words, "the first articulate singer." Besides "Vagabond Lover," Vallee's most memorable hit was "As Time Goes By," which he recorded and released in 1933—nearly a decade before the movie *Casablanca* made the song a classic.

By the 1930s, the crooning style had been totally absorbed into popular American music. Radio and, later, television helped the crooners to become house-hold names. In addition to Bing Crosby, who had established himself long before the Great Depression, there was only one true contender for the title of top crooner of the early thirties. Russ Columbo (1908–1934) released his first and greatest hit, "You Call It Madness (But I Call It Love)," in 1931. Described by many as a Valentino look-alike, Columbo was able to piece together work as a bit actor in movies and orchestral work as a violinist before gaining national attention as a crooner. By the age of twenty-one, Columbo had worked with most of the orchestras in Los Angeles and had appeared in small roles in a handful of movies.

Due to the sudden illness of the regular singer on a live CBS radio broadcast from the Hotel Roosevelt, Columbo made his way to the microphone for the first time. His instant success with listeners led to his working as a standby for the star vocalist of the Gus Arnheim Band—none other than Bing Crosby. Crosby left the band after a tiff with a club manager, and Columbo, his future rival for the hearts of American music lovers, took center stage.

After a national tour with the Arnheim band, Russ returned to California and formed his own successful group, after which Hollywood movie moguls soon started offering him meatier roles. The following year, however, Colombo was killed in a freak accident when a friend struck a match on an antique dueling pistol he had been using as a paperweight. The gun turned out to be loaded and somehow fired, and the ricocheting bullet hit Columbo in the head.

Other crooners of the thirties, such as Dick Powell (1904–1963), Ozzie Nelson (1932–1975), and Jack Leonard, also made their mark in popular music, but Bing remained unrivaled in national attention for the rest of the decade.

Swing

Although the big band had only recently come into being, the jazz tradition of continually reinventing the music brought about the rise of a new style called swing. Until the birth of this style's rhythmic vocabulary and its reintroduction of scat singing, the validity of jazz as an art form was still being questioned by nearly everyone (including important black intellectuals of the Harlem Renaissance, such as Paul Robeson).

The birth of swing can be placed in 1932 with Ivie Anderson (1905–1949) singing Duke Ellington's "It Don't Mean A Thing (If It Ain't Got That Swing)," pre-dating swing as a national craze by nearly three years. The swing era, which lasted until about 1944, was the densest period of vocal jazz performance in mainstream American music history.

Although Duke Ellington was notorious for hiring eccentric or even mediocre singers, his inclusion of vocalist Ivie Anderson as his band's central female singer was never questioned by musicians or critics throughout her decade-long tenure with his orchestra.

Ivie Anderson (1905–1949)

Born on July 10, 1905, outside of Oakland, California, Ivie Anderson would, in her brief forty-five years, become the greatest singer of the most successful and groundbreaking band in the history of jazz—the Duke Ellington Orchestra.

Anderson began her career in entertainment as a dancer in a white vaudeville show headlined by Mamie Smith. By the end of the 1920s, Ivie had also toured as a singer, headlining at both the New York and Los Angeles Cotton Clubs. She soon became the first black female singer to front an all-white big band when she sang for Anson Weeks and His Orchestra at the Mark Hopkins Hotel in San Francisco. She later moved to Chicago, where she had a yearlong engagement with Earl Hines and His Orchestra at the Grand Terrace.

Ellington caught Anderson's performance at the Terrace in February 1931 and immediately signed her out from under Earl "Fatha" Hines (1905–1983). As the story goes, Ivie didn't think she was good enough to be with the already near-legendary Duke, and only took the job after much reassurance from Ellington himself.

After eleven years and a Los Angeles appearance in Ellington's musical *Jump For Joy*, Anderson left the orchestra forever, unable to continue touring due to acute asthma. Her recording and performing career after that was sporadic, and she appeared only occasionally in California and Mexico City.

With her singing mostly behind her, Anderson turned her attention to the running of the Chicken Shack, a restaurant she owned with her first husband, Marques Neal, and later to running a real estate business with her second husband, Walter Collins.

"They still talk about Ivie," Ellington said a decade after the end of Anderson's career with his band, "and every girl singer we've had since has had to try to prevail over the Ivie Anderson image."

Acute asthma took its final toll on December 28, 1949. Anderson died without leaving a will, leading to an extensive legal battle between her two former husbands.

After leaving Ellington's stable of musicians, Ivie went into virtual retirement from the music business, recording only once, for Charles Mingus.

Jimmy Rushing, nicknamed Mr. Five by Five because of his tremendous girth, is widely considered to be one of the greatest jazz singers of all time.

Two innovative male artists of the era who were more than Bing soundalikes were Leo Watson (1898–1950) and Jimmy Rushing. The two served the cause of scat while fueling the future of male singers of jazz to come.

Kansas City, Kansas, native Leo Watson, along with his vocal-ukelele group The Spirits of Rhythm, nearly single-handedly established 52nd Street as the hub of jazz in New York City. After the band's breakup in 1936, Artie Shaw and Gene Krupa both hired Watson for short stints with their bands. At the insistence of the Andrews Sisters, Decca finally signed him to a solo recording contract, but bouts with mental illness kept Watson from ever landing on his feet. Rumors of substance abuse, arrests for public indecency, and a twenty-four-hour-long interpretive drum solo during one of New York's race riots ultimately landed him in a mental institution. He died in Los Angeles from pneumonia in 1950.

Jimmy Rushing was the product of an extremely musical family. His father was a professional trumpet player, his mother a respected gospel singer, and his uncle, who may have had the greatest influence on him, brought home a basketful of money each night he'd made as a musician in the red light district of his hometown, Oklahoma City, Oklahoma.

From his early work with Walter Page's Blue Devils to his solo albums on Vanguard and Columbia in 1956, Rushing became a leader among male jazz singers.

Female Swing Singers

The most famous of the female jazz vocalists made their appearances in the first five years of the swing era. The immortal Ella Fitzgerald (1918–1996), singing with Chick Webb's Orchestra, took "scat" to new heights, while Billie Holiday

The fearless Ella Fitzgerald is easily the most important female singer in the history of jazz. Not only did she direct Chick Webb's band after his death, but she went on to create and define, almost single-handedly, the vocalist's role in bebop, the new musical territory explored and mapped out by the inimitable Dizzy Gillespie.

(1915–1959) played a large role in the evolution of women singers from merely popular props of the big band to legitimate solo artists.

From her legendary tracks with Louis Armstrong to her early recordings with another immortal Louis named Jordan, Fitzgerald participated heavily in the recording of jazz duets. Her collaboration with Jordan occurred very early in her career—sometime between 1935 and 1937—and produced the memorable "Petootie Pie."

Several other prominent singers of 1935 shared not only the times and music, but, strangely enough, the same first name. Helen Rowland, Helen Ward, Helen Forrest, Helen Humes (1913–1981), and Helen O'Connell were all integral members of the second round of successful and talented female jazz singers.

Helen Rowland and Helen Ward shared the honor of being the first of the Helens. Rowland toured and recorded with bandleaders Fred Rich and Freddy Martin, while Ward became the first of several Benny Goodman canaries and later toured regularly

Helen Humes (1913–1981)

The recording career of Helen Humes began in 1927, when she was fourteen. The material that Humes chose to sing, much like the story she preferred to tell of her "boring" life, finally alluded to a naughtier side. Throughout her career, the self-described "sweet and lucky" Miss Humes was arrested for gambling, lost several fortunes on the horses, and polished off a bottle of whiskey before every recording date.

Humes never admitted to any of the events of her darker side: "They'll never want to film the story of my life. I came from a happy family....People don't like to hear about you when it's all happiness and contentment—you have to be drug [sic] through the mud and you have to be standing on the corner. But all I know is the good things in life."

More often than not her songs were about sex. "Do What You Did Last Night," part of her earliest recording session, has the audience believing for nearly half of the cut that the girl singing is angelic, but by the beginning of the second verse her language becomes more suggestive, and finally, by the end of the song, downright demanding.

After Helen's first session, Humes's mother thought it was best that she finish high school, which she did before joining tenor saxophonist Al Sears (1910–1990) on a tour of Buffalo, Cincinnati, and New York City. When the group disbanded, Humes and Sears joined Vernon Andrade's Renaissance Ballroom Orchestra. Count Basie (1904–1984) heard her work with Sears and signed her to front his band. Humes took the place of Billie Holiday and stayed with the band for four years. Her work with Basie on the Okeh label consists mostly of blues material, heavily laden with the ever-present Humes double-entendre.

After leaving Basie's band, Humes recorded on Savoy, Decca, and then Aladdin Records. Her style of songs took a turn toward early rhythm and blues ("blues and jump," as it was then called), and in 1945 she had her greatest hit, "E-Baba-Le-Ba."

At the end of the 1950s, Humes returned to jazz with Red Norvo's Orchestra and then with composer-arranger Marty Paich. With interest in her career waning, she attempted her first comeback, traveling to Australia and France. Unfortunately, the tour was financially unsuccessful.

After her mother died in 1967, Humes grew tired of the music business and went to work in a munitions factory in Louisville, Kentucky. After six years of avoiding the music scene, she appeared at the Newport Jazz Festival. Interest in her work again mounted, leading to a gig at the famous New York club the Cookery in 1975 and to her first recording ever on a major label—*It's the Talk of the Town,* on CBS Records. A *New York Times* review of the album was headed, "Helen Humes Discovered Again at 63."

Her largest body of work from any single period in her life came in her sixties, when she began recording for various English, French, and American labels. In 1981, five years after her successful comeback, Humes passed away.

In 1938 Helen Humes replaced Billie Holiday as singer for the Count Basie Orchestra.

with Gene Krupa's band. Helen Ward's exuberant style inspired soundalikes such as Martha Tilton (b. 1918) and Edythe Wright, who at different times replaced Ward in Benny Goodman's band.

Credited with being the most prolific of the Helens, Helen Humes sang six distinctly different styles of music, including jazz. Her study of the blues translated into both popular and eclectic styles of popular music. Humes was one of very few singers to stage a successful comeback after a lenghty hiatus.

The last reigning Helen of swing was the sultry Helen Forrest. Although she cut several sides with Artie Shaw, her work didn't achieve national prominence until World War II, when homesick GIs in love with her songs and voice made Forrest one of the most successful big band singers near the end of the swing era.

Another star to rise during the swing era was Lena Horne (b. 1917), who at sixteen made her first appearance as a chorus girl at the Cotton Club. She was soon taken under the wing of Noble Sissle. Charlie Barnet also recognized the beautiful

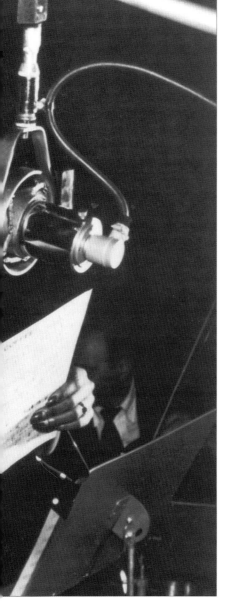

Horne's singing talent and hired her to tour with his troupe. Her work in *Thousands Cheer, Stormy Weather, Ziegfeld Follies,* and Harold Arlen and E.Y. Harburg's *Jamaica* remain classics of movie musical history. In 1981 Horne appeared in *Lena Horne: The Lady and Her Music,* an autobiographical one-woman play. Her most recent stage appearance was a 1994 concert at Carnegie Hall.

No doubt one of the most powerful voices of the entire history of jazz came into the limelight during the swing heyday. Sarah Vaughan (1924–1990) took the art of vocal jazz to new heights by incorporating some of the qualities of crooning, opera, and "clean" improvisation into the female vocalist's repertoire.

Sarah Vaughan at work in the studio recording her collection of Gershwin tunes.

Billy Eckstine (1914–1993) and Sarah Vaughan

In 1942, from the stage of the legendary Apollo Theater, an amateur singer named Sarah Vaughan thrilled her first New York audience with the sounds of a new and vital school of vocal jazz. Her youthful voice embraced the ideals of art and beauty, and her warm, suggestive tones expressed the lyric's meaning while valuing every note. Young and yet refined, Sarah Vaughan captured the heart of every listener from that night forward.

The daughter of a carpenter and a laundress, Sarah "Sassy" Vaughan began as a singer for Mt. Zion Baptist Church in her hometown of Newark, New Jersey. Her technical training in music began at the age of six with studies on the piano and organ. But until that first night at the Apollo (at the age of nineteen) her musical work was solely for the enjoyment of herself and her small community.

In attendance by chance that first evening at the Apollo, vocal master Billy Eckstine recognized that Vaughan not only possessed a great gift but was also perfectly suited to work with him. In her, he recognized elements of his own style, from her inherent technical virtuosity to her recognition of the general audience's melodic sensibilities. It seemed from the very start that the two were destined to sing together.

Their chance to do so occurred nearly overnight. With an introduction to Earl "Fatha" Hines, for whom Eckstine was then singing, Vaughan made her professional debut as both a singer and second pianist in April 1943 with Hines's orchestra. The following year, when Eck-

Bandleader and singer extraordinaire Billy Eckstine is credited with giving Sarah Vaughan her entrance into professional singing.

Together again: Eckstine and Vaughan performing as strongly as ever in the 1980s.

stine left Hines's band to form his own, Vaughan followed. Her first recording session was with Eckstine's group for Continental Records on December 31, 1944.

Eckstine came from a middle-class family in Pittsburgh that valued education. Upon graduation from Armstrong High School in Washington, D.C., Billy began studying at Howard University. After two years of working as a singer and emcee at clubs around Buffalo and Chicago, he gained the attention of Earl "Fatha" Hines. His work with Vaughan a year and a half later with his own small combo turned out to be more short-lived than the band itself, which disintegrated in 1947. In 1945 Vaughan left Eckstine and his orchestra and began a solo career. At the urging of Dizzy Gillespie (1917–1993) and Charlie Parker (1920–1955), she soon landed a contract with Musicraft Records.

Eckstine went on to become leader of a big band that many jazz critics consider to have been well ahead of its time. His incredible orchestra included Dizzy Gillespie, Fats Navarro (1923–1950), Miles Davis (1926–1991), Charlie Parker, and Art Blakey (1919–1990). With the end of the union strikes (see page 38) in 1948, however, Eckstine had to bow to the inevitable, and he began to sing mostly ballads, which at the time were the mainstay of the commerical music industry.

Vaughan didn't recieve widespread recognition until the following year, 1949, when she signed with Columbia, an enormous recording company that was able to provide her exposure on international radio and television. American jazz fans hailed her as the most important singer of the era. *Downbeat* magazine's poll, from 1947 to 1952, crowned her the greatest female singer in jazz.

Eckstine also met with critical acclaim, winning the *Downbeat* polls from 1949 to 1954. But due to the poor recording techniques allowed him by his label during the era, his recordings haven't weathered the test of time as well as Vaughan's. "Sassy" continued to record up until her death in 1990.

STRIKES OF THE 1940s

The end of the big band era had less to do with the changing musical tastes of Americans than it did with the 1943 and 1948 musicians' union strikes. In an attempt to get a fair share of the profits made off the labor of working musicians, employees of all bands began working together to fight the record industry, whose profits never made it back to the pockets of those who had performed on the projects. Although the workers' concerns were legitimate—that their work was part of the profit-making process and should be financially rewarded— the long-term demise of the product's quality and the apparent end of artist-driven music were the two most lasting effects of the battle between musicians, songwriters, and the recording industry.

The American Society of Composers, Authors and Publishers (ASCAP) and the American Federation of Musicians (AFM) began to wage war against the industry's business practices. Their greatest weapon, bans and strikes, ultimately backfired; they disenfranchised the legitimate musician while leading to a growth of power in the recording industry. The labels went from being merely archivists of the times to being the makers of music history.

By changing their focus from scouting for the greatest talent to finding the greatest market, the record industry ultimately won not only the union battle, but also the popular music war. To this day, American music directly reflects the union's

Pearl Bailey recorded duets with several artists, including Hot Lips Page, Frank Sinatra, and comedienne Moms Mabley.

Dinah Shore was just setting out on her singing career when the strikes came.

mishandling of the situation. The union was dependent upon musicians en masse refusing to give in until their demands were met. The problem the AFM faced was that it only protected those musicians working in established big bands, clubs, and on Broadway. The majority of up-and-coming musicians trying to break into the business were not at the negotiating table.

ASCAP suffered from a two-fold problem. Not only was their membership exclusive, like the AFM, but they had a main competitor vying for the right to make profits off of the songs of composers—BMI (Broadcast Music Inc.). When ASCAP struck, the recording industry simply went to the union's competition. ASCAP did make some gains in the struggle concerning royalties, and the AFM settled with each label separately and at different times during 1943 and 1944.

Music in general ultimately suffered most from the rise of the artist & repertory (A&R) man. These free agents were able to take the pressure off the labels by engineering a change from artist-driven to market-driven music without involving the business's bureaucrats. Direct responsibility for the relationship between artists and the labels changed hands to a third party—the A&R man—who no longer needed to negotiate with the powerful bandleaders. The A&R representative found power in controlling the less-than-business-minded singers and the material they covered.

Very few of the big-band jazz singers were able to make the transition with their ego and craft intact. Each singer now had to deal with the pressures that came with contract negotiations. Few dared to risk their place on a major label, and the result was the virtual disappearance of great songs and great instrumental musicians.

The singers who wished to follow the evolution of jazz, the music that had made them stars only a decade before, faced obscurity on minor labels and minimal financial success. Those who did succumb to the pressures of the A&R men, the singers for whom financial insecurity meant their families would suffer, were forced to record inane tunes that made a quick dollar but ultimately ruined their long-term credibility.

The perception problem that Bing Crosby has had since the forties is due in part to the tunes he handled after the strike. With fifty-eight songs still unissued before the strike, Crosby was able to ride out the situation. But once on the other side of the strike, short-term marketing ploys bilked Bing of his respectable place in American music history. Ditties like "Pistol Packin' Mama" and "Don't Fence Me In" were catchy like the flu, but offered little in terms of artistic innovation. However, the generation raised on Bing remained loyal and continued to buy his records through the fifties, ignoring the silliness of the songs laid down by Bing the Cowboy and Santa Bing.

Dick Haymes (1916–1980), thought by some to be the greatest balladeer of the forties, was ultimately ostracized by the business arm of the music. Personal problems, which included a fight over his wife (Rita Hayworth Haymes) with the executive producer of

Santa Bing (a promo shot for his album *White Christmas*). Crosby was able to remain successful as a singer for four decades primarily because of his ability to wear many hats, musically speaking.

Decca, brought promotion of his work to a halt after 1956, relegating him to permanent obscurity.

The brightest male star to emerge from the union rubble was Francis Sinatra (b. 1915). Fresh from the Tommy Dorsey band, Sinatra recorded "Sunday, Monday or Always," a tune that Bing covered for his 1943 movie, *Dixie*. The song, which was supposed to be a sure-fire hit for Crosby, was scooped out from under him during the ban by Sinatra. Frank's discography from that early post-ban period to his last gold record in 1993 is a history of crooning in itself.

In 1944 Dinah Shore's (and Perry Como's) label, Victor, was the last house to settle with the AFM. Shore (1917–1994), who had only recently gained some notoriety

Trumpeter, singer, bandleader, and native Texan Oran "Hot Lips" Page, who sang a duet with Pearl Bailey, died in New York City at the age of 46.

prior to the ban, was able to hit the charts in 1944 with "Tess's Torch Song." Like other women of the era, Doris Day (b. 1922) was allowed to record in the jazz idiom between "high-pop" ditties. Some of Day's greatest work came from recording with a trio from the Harry James group. The album *Young Man with a Horn* (Columbia, 1950) shows off Day's tremendous virtuosity.

Like singer Pearl Bailey, some former jazz performers who braved commercial music post-ban met, surprisingly, with economic success as well as professional longevity. Of Bailey's duets, the most memorable was with singer-trumpeter Hot Lips Page (1908–1954). The pair recorded a duet version of "The Hucklebuck," a song based on a saxophone solo by Charlie Parker and recorded by dozens of artists since the 1940s.

Nat "King" Cole (1917–1965)

Nat "King" Cole hit the charts for the first time in 1943 with "Straighten Up and Fly Right," thus beginning an ascent toward superstardom. By the end of his all-too-brief life, Cole had amassed an international following that was virtually unrivaled.

onward, Cole rarely made full use of his enormous skills at the piano, deciding instead to take front and center as a vocalist. Like Crosby, he covered some pretty uninspired tunes after the ban, but his performance was always immaculate.

Among many other firsts, Nat "King" Cole was the first African-American with his own television series.

Knowledgeable in both music and business, Cole was able to make the transition from jazz to pop music following the bans. As the pianist and leader of his own trio before the union strikes, Cole refocused his efforts soon after, and began envisioning himself as a pop icon rather than a jazz performer. From 1948

Nat "King" Cole became the first African-American to star in his own television show, and the first to live in Beverly Hills. Cole hit the charts for the last time in 1989 when his daughter Natalie (b. 1950) recorded a posthumous duet of "Unforgettable." Nat "King" Cole died of cancer in 1965.

BEBOP

The rift between pop and jazz, which began with the ASCAP and AFM strikes of the forties, was in many ways a liberating experience for jazz instrumentalists, who had watched their craft become bureaucratically compartmentalized nearly out of existence.

Reminiscing: Sammy Davis, Jr., Dizzy Gillespie, Sarah Vaughan, and Billy Eckstine entertain a television audience with fond memories of the golden days of jazz.

Many of the musicians who followed the path of jazz from 1944 on made their way into bebop. Still aware of the audience and the role of entertainment, bebop engaged the intellect of its fine players without losing its sense of humor. A hybrid of Latin and African musics (which was hinted at by the work of Charlie Parker and brought to life by his friend and colleague Dizzy Gillespie) bebop was a welcome challenge to composers and musicians who wished to continue experimenting with rhythm, mode, and tone. Melody was no longer driven by the boundaries of the human voice, but by the piano, drums, and horns. Instrumental dexterity and technical complexity defined the form.

The advances made in melodic structure by the bop generation were driven primarily by the elimination of the voice as the centerpiece of the song. This instrument-driven style inevitably led to an evolution in singing. The name itself, "be-bop," suggests the vocal language that emerged from the movement. "Oop-Pop-A-Da" and "In the Land of Oo-Bla-De" are examples of songs structured around nonsensical syllabic vocal phrasing that mimicked instrumental solos.

Out of Dizzy Gillespie's band came several of the successful scat singers who made the transition from swing to bebop, including Joe Carroll (1919–1981) and Kenny "Pancho" Hagood, two of the earliest singers to attempt vocals in the bop style, and the undisputed queen of bop, Ella Fitzgerald.

Each of these singers credited Leo Watson for their shared scat styles. Humor, among Leo Watson's greatest gifts, became the audience-legitimizing factor for be-bop. Having a good time on stage took the edge off the insanity of super-human vo-calizing and instrumentation. Dave Lambert (1917–1966), Buddy Stewart (1921–1950), and Ella Fitzgerald were witty as well as virtuosic leaders of the new school.

Ella Fitzgerald used a combination of humor and virtuosity to thrill her audiences.

Ella Fitzgerald (1918–1996) and Louis Armstrong (1900–1971)

Throughout the brief history of jazz, very few performers have been accepted by audiences and critics alike as both artists and entertainers. At the very top of that slim category sit Ella Fitzgerald and

Ella Fitzgerald and Louis Armstrong, pictured here discussing material in the recording studio, performed dozens of songs together on record, the best of which can be found in the two-volume set *Ella and Louis Again.*

Louis Armstrong. The two of them came together in 1957 to record a substantial number of memorable duets, which were compiled in a two-volume collection called *Ella and Louis Again,* released by Verve.

The Virginia-born Ella Fitzgerald began her career as the first of many important winners of the Apollo Theater talent contest in New York City. Thanks to her extensive knowledge of popular melodies and the know-how to randomly incorporate those tunes into any song she might cover, Fitzgerald redefined scat singing.

At the age of seventeen, following her win at the Apollo, Ella enjoyed her first professional success with "A-Tisket A-Tasket," her first hit as the canary for the Chick Webb Orchestra. Four years later, Webb died of tuberculosis, and leadership of the band fell to Ella, at the ripe age of twenty-one. She

remained as the leader of the band for two years before beginning her solo career.

By 1945 Fitzgerald had established herself as the country's preeminent scat singer. Her solo hit "Flying Home" incorporated familiar jazz instrumental solos as part of her vocal riffs.

Ella was the first female singer to brave the strange new terrain of bebop. She began touring with Dizzy Gillespie's band in the mid-forties, and honed her ever-expanding vocal chops to include the new harmonies being experimented with in bebop. The leading bass player of the new form, Ray Brown, married Fitzgerald in 1947.

In the early 1950s, Fitzgerald signed a recording contract with Decca and produced some of her most popular albums. The lack of good new material brought to her at the beginning of her career with Decca led to her request to record the best songs of the best composers of Broadway. Decca bowed to her request for only a short while, which eventually led to her departure from the company.

Between her recordings on Decca and those on her next label, Verve, Fitzgerald recorded dozens of showtune albums. *Ella Sings Gershwin, The Cole Porter Songbook, The Rodgers and Hart Songbook, Irving Berlin, The Gershwin Songbook,* and *Hello*

Dolly! are all two-record sets containing thirty songs each. Nearly every cut on each of these albums is considered the definitive jazz version of a Broadway hit.

Like Fitzgerald, New Orleans native Louis Armstrong incorporated show tunes into his repertoire. By doing so, "Satchmo" (a moniker he took on after a European critic muddled his original nickname, "Satchelmouth") contributed to the success of some of Broadway's most popular musicals. Two recordings in particular had a tremendous impact. When Armstrong's renditions of "Mack the Knife" and "Hello Dolly!" were released and went straight to the top of the music charts, ticket sales for Brecht and Weill's *Three Penny Opera* and for *Hello Dolly!* doubled practically overnight.

On top of his recording credits for songs from musicals, Armstrong also fell into work as an actor and singer on the Broadway stage. His first appearance came in 1929 with *Hot Chocolates,* a broadway revue for which he played trumpet before being called to the stage on a whim during one evening's performance. From that day forward, Armstrong took to the stage each night for his rendition of the show's hit song "(What Did I Do to Be So) Black and Blue." He again took to the Great White Way in 1939 with the jazz musical version of Shakespeare's *A Midsummer Night's Dream,* entitled *Swingin' the Dream.* The show, thanks in large part to the hit song "Darn That Dream," was so popular that it was made into a movie starring Armstrong and Billie Holiday.

More than any other jazz artist, Louis Armstrong can be credited with the mounting popularity of jazz between 1920 and 1950.

VOCALESE

The next logical step after scat (the singing of nonsensical syllabic phrases) was the addition of a lyric story line to the instrumentally influenced vocal solo. Although this concept, called "vocalese", was tested very early on in jazz, it took audiences a number of years before they would embrace the "lyricizing" of an instrumental solo line.

By 1939 Leo Watson was experimenting with lyrics placed over existing sixteen-bar solo lines. Eddie Jefferson (1918–1979) carved the first successful path to vocalese as early as 1941, and in 1945 Dave Lambert and Buddy Stewart made their attempts at vocalese and in the process made a name for themselves performing duets. Despite these musical successes, the vocalese school was not accepted by audiences until Sarah Vaughan and Eddie Jefferson teamed up in 1950 for "Beautiful Memories." In 1951 King Pleasure scored a vocalese hit with "Moody Mood for Love."

The fickle relationship Americans have had with vocalese stems from the fact that few qualified singers made the style a practice, and therefore it was never polished into an art. With Dave Lambert, however, the preeminent vocalese artist, the craft of lyrics over solo lines found a life-long practitioner.

The dapper King Pleasure was one of the first artists to popularize vocalese, a school of singing based on singing lyrics over formerly instrumental solos.

Vocalese's third and greatest incarnation came with the introduction of Dave Lambert to composer-arranger Jon Hendricks and singer Annie Ross. Their album *Everybody's Boppin'* brought the concept of vocal jazz trios back to the limelight. Not since the Boswell Sisters and the Mills Brothers of the 1930s had the tight harmony and rhythmic complexity of multiple jazz voicings been as successful as it was with Lambert, Hendricks & Ross.

Annie Ross (b. 1930)

At the age of four, Annie Ross and her aunt Ella Logan moved to Hollywood, California, from Surrey, England, so that the child singer and actress could make headway into the motion-picture industry. At the age of eight, Ross starred in *Our Gang Follies of 1938*. She followed up that

the time, on drums. Hits from that session, such as "Moody's Mood for Love" and "Twisted," brought her to the attention of Dave Lambert and Jon Hendricks.

Before true success could catch up to her, however, Ross returned to Europe to tour with Lionel Hampton's band. After a fight with Hampton in Sweden, Ross left for London, where she landed a starring role in the hit revue *Cranks*.

Thanks to this theatrical success, Lambert and Hendricks finally made a

Although she was an influential recording artist in her own right, Annie Ross is best remembered for her work as a member of the vocal trio Lambert, Hendricks & Ross.

appearance with a role playing Judy Garland's sister in *Presenting Lily Mars*. At sixteen, she began studying in New York at the American Academy of Dramatic Arts.

At odds with her aunt, Ross left for London, where she soon found work in the West End's theater district. Within a year, however, she moved to Paris, spending the majority of her time hanging out with the ever-growing number of expatriate American jazz musicians. Ross laid down her first recordings with a Parisian jazz group led by James Moody.

During a visit to New York, Ross cut her first album for DeeGee Records (Dizzy's short-lived label), accompanied by Blossom Dearie on piano, members of the Modern Jazz Quartet, and Kenny Clarke, her boyfriend at

real effort to work with her. After several failed recording sessions with Ross as the choral coach of an all-women's jazz singing group, the three decided to try their voices as a trio. The recordings that Lambert, Hendricks & Ross made over the following few years placed them among the top three jazz vocal groups of all times.

The trio of Lambert, Hendricks & Ross was originally a quartet, with singer and actress Georgia Brown (1933–1992) as the soprano. Ross apparently told Georgia Brown that the rest of the group wanted her out. Georgia left town without saying goodbye. Only years later did Dave Lambert discover that Annie had forced Brown out of the group because she "wanted to be the only woman of the group."

UO-COOL

During an era defined by the freneticism of "hot" jazz, there arose a school of musicians whose personalities demanded a different musical temperament. The songs covered by this new breed of musicians, from ballads to faster-paced swing numbers, differed from those of the "hot" players only in interpretation. Following the lead of earlier players such as Bix Beiderbecke and Lester Young (1909–1959), the musicians of the new cool school placed their emphasis on the instrument's tone and its relationship to the player's personality.

The birth of popular cool came on September 1948 at New York's Royal Roost club when the former trumpet player for Charlie Parker, Miles Davis, led his group in an evening of music that was more introspective than anything that had previously been explored by bebop or swing. This performance helped usher in a new era in jazz that

The sexy and talented Anita O'Day recounted her drug-filled life in music in her autobiography
Hard Times, High Times.

Chet Baker, once a strikingly handsome young man, aged quickly and badly thanks to decades of heroin addiction. When Baker once told a fellow trumpeter that all the marks on his face were laugh lines, the sideman replied, "Nothing's that funny."

redefined both instrumental and vocal interpretation.

By the mid-fifties, the singers who had nearly been eliminated by the instrumental advances of bebop found a new home in cool. What made the new cool singers different from their bebop counterparts was subtlety. A subtle vocal phrase meant more than flashy, superhuman vocal feats. After an era of singers such as Billy Eckstine and Sarah Vaughan, whose crafts were based on the beauty of embellishment, the newest breed of singers stayed away from vocal frivolities. The vibrato—the key element to most crooning—was virtually eliminated. The emphasis was placed primarily on vocal dynamics and clarity of pitch.

Trumpeter Chet Baker (1929–1988) led the vo-cool era with the release of his ten-inch LP *Chet Baker Sings*. Although his choices were spare, his vocal tone was suggestive and provocative. Throughout his life and career with Capitol Records, Baker was one of the most popular cool jazz performers.

The history of the successful female vo-cool singers begins with June Christy (1925–1990) and her 1954 hit song, "Something Cool." The single proved so successful that Capitol decided to build an album around the song. By 1956 the album *Something Cool* had sold more than 93,000 copies. Christy's simple, melancholy vocal style made the cheeriest of songs seem to be steeped in hard-won wisdom.

In 1954 Anita O'Day (b. 1919), a singer whose work had previously been released only on minor labels, surfaced as the female leader of the cool movement. O'Day's rough-and-tumble lifestyle, as illustrated by her frank autobiography *Hard Times, High Times,* was apparent in her interpretations of jazz standards. O'Day abandoned the melody almost entirely, risking everything for the sake of personal freedom through interpretation. Her consistently high-energy performances, in tandem with flights into melodic space, left audiences on the edge of their seats, curious as to whether she'd make it through the material in one piece. The beauty of O'Day's style relied on the fact that she nearly always pulled off her wild musical choices.

Mel Tormé (b. 1925)

One of the all-time greats of male jazz singing, Mel Tormé, had his greatest impact by melding his versatile scat skills with the casual tone that gave the vo-cool movement life. A native of Chicago, Tormé began his show-biz career as a child actor on radio spots and, a littler later on, in the movies. His earliest singing job larity machine, forced Tormé to focus his work on more substantial material and move away from his contract with Capitol. For the sake of greater artistic control, he began taking tremendous pay cuts to work on smaller, more artistically inclined labels.

The vo-cool movement has Tormé's artistic decision to thank for some of its great-

Early in his career, Mel Tormé collaborated briefly with Peggy Lee.

came with Chico Marx's all-juvenile dance-band orchestra, a group put together by producers to pay off Chico's gambling debts.

Prior to enlisting in the army during World War II, Tormé led a vocal group called the Mel-Tones, which recorded on both Jewell and Decca Records. After he rejoined the group at the end of the war, the trio signed with Musicraft and began a journey into modern jazz.

Tormé's singing and acting career continued with Capitol and MGM respectively after the demise of the Mel-Tones. Resentment within the music community over the unbelievable success of Tormé's lesser works, along with Mel's own disgust with the popu-est music. His work on the Bethlehem label is some of the finest music of the decade. Albums such as *Mel Tormé and the Marty Paich Dek-Tette* and *Mel Tormé Sings Fred Astaire* show off his ability to reconstruct any well-known tune and make it seem new again. Still on top of his remarkable vocal chops, Tormé remains an exceptional arranger and composer whose overall abilities would have been lost on the bigger music labels.

From his brief work as a singer of duets, the most notable collaboration was with Cleo Laine (b. 1927), a British singer and actress well known in her homeland for her incredible range and scat abilities.

Not everyone who'd decided upon the path of most resistance (a life in jazz after the strikes) made the transition into vo-cool or bebop. Some of the most popular big bands survived for a decade or more after the music's heyday. During the fifties, Keely Smith (b. 1932) and husband and bandleader Louis Prima (1911–1978) continued to be successful in Chicago, New York, and Los Angeles performing nostalgic songs of the thirties and forties. The Count Basie Orchestra had a renaissance of sorts during the fifties thanks to the popularity of singer Joe Williams.

Husband and wife Louis Prima and Keely Smith shared responbility for their own record label, Keelou, during the late fifties and early sixties.

CONCLUSION

Throughout the 1950s, the A&R man continued the tireless search for the greatest music market, and soon discovered that teenagers represented a prime "target market," one that regularly bought more albums by far than any other age group in America. By focusing on this group's juvenile desires and scant musical education, the industry once again redefined popular American music while turning (of course) a healthy profit. The relationship between pop music and jazz, which had been growing more strained for over a decade, was finally and completely severed.

Three elements the music of the younger generation still shared with the tunes of their parents were the singer as the "front" person of the band, the basic A-A-B-A song structure, and the rhythmic possibility for dance. A fourth and key ingredient to the "new" pop, which legitimized the transition in the ears of consumers, was the use of the blues scale.

In the fifties, Frank Sinatra's crown as the greatest male singer in America was passed to Elvis Presley (1935–1977), whose Delta blues–derived sound and youthful, brash style spoke to the newly discovered youth market. Frank and Elvis had in common the same historical vocal traits of the blues-based crooning balladeer.

Like Presley, a brash southern singer named Brenda Lee (b. 1944) grabbed the torch of female popular singing from the likes of Doris Day and Dinah Shore. While Lee did sing many popular ballads, the vocal similarities between the women who bridged the gap in popular music are fewer than those between Sinatra and Presley. The jazz-influenced songs of the forties had finally lost out to the combination of country music and rhythm and blues that would soon evolve into rock and roll.

Brenda Lee, appealing primarily to the youth market, represented the final break between pop music and jazz.

The most important musical elements lost in the transition to rock and roll were the crafts of orchestral arrangement, intricate vocal technique, and the instrumental vocabulary that had been built upon, one musician at a time, over the first half of the twentieth century. Faced more than ever with financial ruin and artistic obscurity, the musicians who continued to hone their craft in jazz engaged in a tumultuous, music-driven debate over the content of jazz and the direction of its future.

Instrumental musicians still interested in the evolution of the music focused on the expansion of song form and scale. Miles Davis continued to commandeer, shape, and define that future with groundbreaking albums such as *Kind of Blue*, which introduced listeners to preeminent players John Coltrane (1926–1967), Cannonball Adderley (1928–1975), Bill Evans (1929–1980), Paul Chambers (1935–1969), and James Cobb (b. 1929).

The elimination of the human voice was, in this school of jazz, permanent. Instrumental music's vocabulary continued to expand throughout the fifties, moving farther away from preconceived notions of melody. The idea of human evolution through musical innovation drove the music toward the avant-garde. Along with Coltrane, several "out" players (a term used in jazz to imply the move away from conventional form) emerged, changing the relationship between performers and audience forever. Archie Shepp (b. 1937), Ornette Coleman (b. 1930), and, later on, Cecil Taylor (b. 1929) and Bill Dixon (b. 1925) created a music that was not interested in providing widely accessible entertainment.

A huge star of the British popular music scene during the seventies, jazz singer, pianist, and activist Nina Simone resettled in France after becoming disenchanted with America's political culture.

Abbey Lincoln, a performer who has survived by perpetually reinventing herself, has had many names. Born Anna Marie Woolridge, she has also gone by the names Gaby Lee and Aminata Moseka.

The vo-cool movement of the mid-fifties was able to sustain its top singers only into the early sixties. The jazz singers who emerged after the reign of cool primarily remained true to the music of the "good old days." The songs that began falling under the category of "standard" material were not a part of jazz at all, and had to be revised to fit the idiom. No matter how much pop-jazz singers tried to update and repopularize the music they so loved, the concept of "jazzing up" songs from the fifties and sixties only made more obvious the moribund state of vocal jazz.

Financially unable to sustain a band, many singers accompanied themselves on the piano. Rose Murphy (1913–1989), Nellie Lutcher (b. 1915), Nina Simone (b. 1933), Andy Bey, Blossom Dearie (b. 1928), Dorothy Donegan (b. 1924), Mary McPartland (b. 1920), and Shirley Horn (b. 1934) belonged to an era defined by necessity. If singers were to continue practicing their art, they had to be, for the most part, self-sufficient.

The British Invasion was brought on in part by the fact that Americans were tired of the fight over popular American music. Again, jazz took a staggering blow with the rise of rock, falling a distant third in popularity. With the rise of rock, the number of singers interested in performing jazz—a field that could offer almost no benefits—slipped to almost nil. Those few who did suffer the terrain have made a lasting, possibly final mark on the history of jazz singing.

One jazz vocalist whose rise in popularity came in the midst of the popular drought was Abbey Lincoln (b. 1930). Over a career that has spanned thirty years, Lincoln has reinvented herself several times, into whatever persona she has seen fit. Her rise to respectability and autonomy came with the album *That's Him* (1957), in which she chose to ignore the concept of musical advancement and returned to the sounds of the twenties and thirties, breathing new life into the earliest work of African-American stars such as Ethel Waters and Florence Mills.

Another performer who began her career in the latter days of swing was pianist-singer Carmen McRae (1922–1994). Her greatest successes came in the late fifties with her timeless recordings on Decca: *By Special Request* (1955) and *When You're Away* (1959).

The sixties saw the rise of two important female performers: Peggy Lee (b. 1920) and Betty Carter (b. 1930). While both remained faithful to the Tin Pan Alley song standard, their styles were quite different. Lee tried on many occasions to update the jazz sound to fit the marketing ploys of the current music scene, while Carter remained true to the history of jazz, yet interpreted songs in an innovative near-avant-garde vocal style.

Since the 1960s, there has been no apparent heir to the throne of the jazz-pop vocal school. Those with the vocal dexterity to cover almost any style of music have invariably done so, coming to jazz in the later years of their musical careers, mostly as an homage to the music of the past. One exception to this rule is modern-day crooner Harry Connick, Jr. (b. 1967), who has been playing jazz piano around his hometown of New Orleans since childhood. Connick recently released recordings

Carmen McRae was one of the most beloved jazz singers of the modern age. She continued to perform and record right up to her death at age seventy-two.

Betty Carter's rise to stardom can be attributed partly to the rave reviews she received from the *Village Voice* for her work in theater.

of more pop-oriented material blending the sounds of New Orleans with rock rhythms.

While it may be discouraging to contemplate the current lack of any vital and new vocal jazz movement, this decades-long vacuum has had at least one positive consequence. When today's listeners, hungry for the excitement of vocal jazz, turn to the music of jazz singers such as Ethel Waters and Louis Armstrong or Betty Carter and Harry Connick, Jr., the music that they hear contains a comprehensive aural history of our shared twentieth-century American experience.

Harry Connick, Jr., possibly the last popular crooner of vocal jazz, recorded a duet with Carmen McRae just before her death in 1994.

SUGGESTED LISTENING

Louis Armstrong—*Ella and Louis Again Volume I*
(Verve 825373-2 CD)

Mildred Bailey—*Harlem Lullaby*
(British Living Era ASV CDAJA)

Boswell Sisters—*The Boswell Sisters*
(Patricia Records ApS Denmark CD 23121)

Betty Carter—*'Round Midnight*
(Atco, Japanese Atlantic AMCY–1060)

Doris Day—*Doris Day and Les Brown: Best of the Big Bands*
(Columbia CK-46224)

Ella Fitzgerald—*Duke Ellington*
(Verve, three CDs 837-035-2)

Billie Holiday—*Billie Holiday*, Volumes 1–9
(ARC label, CK-40646, CK-40790, CK-44048, CK-44252, CK-44423, CK-45449, CK- 46180, CK-47030)

Helen Humes—*Count Basie, 1938–1939*
(Classics 504)

King Pleasure—*Golden Days*
(Original Jazz Classics, OJC 1772 CD/LP)

Lambert, Hendricks and Ross—*Everybody's Boppin'*
(Columbia CK-45020)

Abbey Lincoln—*That's Him*
(Riverside, OJCCD-085-2)

Carmen McRae with Dave Brubeck—*Take Five*
(Columbia Special Products A 9116)

Anita O'Day—*Pick Yourself Up*
(POCJ–1940)

Jimmy Rushing—*The Essential Jimmy Rushing*
(Vanguard VCD 65/66 CD)

Dinah Shore—*The Best of Dinah Shore*
(Curb D2-77459)

Jo Stafford—*Collector's Series*
(Capital, CDP7-91638-2)

Kay Starr—*Kay Starr, Collector's Series*
(C27-94888-2)

Dinah Washington—*Dinah Washington, 1943–1945*
(Danish Official label 83004)

Ethel Waters—*On Stage and Screen*
(Columbia Special Products A 2792)

Lee Wiley—*I've Got You Under My Skin: The Complete Young Lee Wiley, 1931–1937*
(Vintage Jazz Classics VJC–1023-2)

FURTHER READING

Collier, James Lincoln. *Jazz: The American Theme Song*. New York: Oxford University Press, Inc., 1992.

Crow, Bill. *From Birdland to Broadway*. New York: Oxford University Press, Inc., 1992.

Feather, Leonard. *The Encyclopedia of Jazz*. New York: Horizon Press, 1960.

Friedwald, Will. *Jazz Singing*. New York: Collier Books, 1992.

Koerner, Julie. *Big Bands* (Life, Times & Music® series). New York: Friedman/Fairfax Publishers, 1992.

Woll, Allen. *Black Musical Theatre, From Coontown to Dreamgirls*. Baton Rouge, La.: Da Capo Press, 1989.

PHOTO CREDITS